50 Meal Prep Recipes for a Healthy Week

By: Kelly Johnson

Table of Contents

- Grilled Chicken and Quinoa Bowls
- Turkey Meatball and Sweet Potato Meal Prep
- Roasted Veggie and Hummus Bowls
- Lemon Garlic Salmon with Brown Rice
- Chicken Fajita Bowls with Cauliflower Rice
- Beef Stir-Fry with Veggies and Brown Rice
- Veggie-Packed Lentil Soup
- Grilled Shrimp and Avocado Salad
- Roasted Chicken with Sweet Potato and Broccoli
- Chickpea and Quinoa Salad
- Tofu Stir-Fry with Veggies
- Zucchini Noodles with Pesto and Chicken
- Grilled Turkey Burgers with Roasted Veggies
- Mediterranean Tuna Salad
- Spaghetti Squash with Turkey Bolognese
- Eggplant and Chickpea Curry
- Asian Chicken Salad with Peanut Dressing
- Beef and Broccoli Stir-Fry with Brown Rice
- Sweet Potato and Black Bean Tacos
- Lemon Herb Grilled Chicken with Asparagus
- Roasted Cauliflower and Lentil Bowls
- Chicken Caesar Salad with Greek Yogurt Dressing
- Sweet Potato and Kale Breakfast Hash
- Grilled Steak and Veggie Skewers
- Quinoa and Black Bean Burrito Bowls
- Spicy Chickpea and Sweet Potato Salad
- Grilled Veggie and Tofu Wraps
- Lemon Basil Chicken with Spinach and Rice
- Peanut Butter Banana Overnight Oats
- Spicy Turkey and Rice Bowls
- Salmon with Roasted Brussels Sprouts
- Baked Falafel with Tzatziki and Cucumber Salad
- Chicken Shawarma Bowls with Hummus
- Zucchini and Turkey Meatloaf
- Grilled Portobello Mushrooms with Quinoa

- Roasted Shrimp and Veggie Buddha Bowls
- Turkey Chili with Quinoa
- Spinach and Ricotta Stuffed Chicken Breast
- Cauliflower Fried Rice with Tofu
- Miso Soup with Tofu and Veggies
- Thai Peanut Chicken with Veggie Noodles
- Roasted Beet Salad with Chickpeas
- Grilled Chicken with Roasted Broccoli and Sweet Potatoes
- Chia Pudding with Almond Butter and Berries
- Veggie and Quinoa Stuffed Peppers
- Sweet Potato and Spinach Salad
- Roasted Lemon Garlic Shrimp with Couscous
- Baked Salmon with Roasted Brussels Sprouts
- Spaghetti Squash Primavera with Grilled Chicken
- Grilled Chicken and Veggie Kabobs

Grilled Chicken and Quinoa Bowls

Ingredients:

- 2 chicken breasts
- 1 cup quinoa, cooked
- 1 tbsp olive oil
- 1 tsp garlic powder
- 1 tsp paprika
- Salt and pepper, to taste
- 1 cup cucumber, diced
- 1 cup cherry tomatoes, halved
- 1 avocado, sliced
- Fresh cilantro, for garnish

Instructions:

1. **Grill chicken** – Season chicken breasts with olive oil, garlic powder, paprika, salt, and pepper. Grill for 6–8 minutes per side, until cooked through.
2. **Prepare quinoa** – Cook quinoa according to package instructions.
3. **Assemble bowls** – In bowls, layer quinoa, grilled chicken (sliced), cucumber, tomatoes, and avocado.
4. **Serve** – Garnish with fresh cilantro and enjoy!

Turkey Meatball and Sweet Potato Meal Prep

Ingredients:

- 1 lb ground turkey
- 1 egg
- 1 tsp garlic powder
- 1 tsp onion powder
- 1 tsp dried oregano
- Salt and pepper, to taste
- 2 medium sweet potatoes, peeled and cubed
- 1 tbsp olive oil
- Fresh parsley, chopped (optional)

Instructions:

1. **Preheat oven** – Set to 400°F (200°C).
2. **Make meatballs** – In a bowl, combine ground turkey, egg, garlic powder, onion powder, oregano, salt, and pepper. Roll into 1-inch meatballs.
3. **Roast sweet potatoes** – Toss sweet potato cubes with olive oil, salt, and pepper. Spread on a baking sheet.
4. **Bake** – Place meatballs on the same baking sheet and bake for 20–25 minutes, until the meatballs are cooked through and sweet potatoes are tender.
5. **Serve** – Portion into meal prep containers and garnish with fresh parsley.

Roasted Veggie and Hummus Bowls

Ingredients:

- 1 zucchini, sliced
- 1 bell pepper, chopped
- 1 red onion, chopped
- 1 tbsp olive oil
- 1 tsp dried thyme
- Salt and pepper, to taste
- 1 cup cooked quinoa or rice
- ½ cup hummus
- Fresh parsley, chopped (optional)

Instructions:

1. **Preheat oven** – Set to 400°F (200°C).
2. **Prepare veggies** – Toss zucchini, bell pepper, and onion with olive oil, thyme, salt, and pepper.
3. **Roast** – Spread vegetables on a baking sheet and roast for 20–25 minutes, until tender and caramelized.
4. **Assemble bowls** – In bowls, add a base of quinoa or rice, then top with roasted veggies and a dollop of hummus.
5. **Serve** – Garnish with fresh parsley and enjoy!

Lemon Garlic Salmon with Brown Rice

Ingredients:

- 2 salmon fillets
- 1 tbsp olive oil
- 2 garlic cloves, minced
- 1 lemon, sliced
- Salt and pepper, to taste
- 1 cup cooked brown rice
- Fresh parsley, for garnish

Instructions:

1. **Preheat oven** – Set to 375°F (190°C).
2. **Prepare salmon** – Place salmon fillets on a baking sheet, drizzle with olive oil, and top with minced garlic and lemon slices.
3. **Bake** – Season with salt and pepper and bake for 15–20 minutes, until salmon flakes easily with a fork.
4. **Serve** – Serve with a side of cooked brown rice and garnish with fresh parsley.

Chicken Fajita Bowls with Cauliflower Rice

Ingredients:

- 2 chicken breasts, sliced into strips
- 1 tbsp olive oil
- 1 tsp cumin
- 1 tsp chili powder
- 1 tsp garlic powder
- Salt and pepper, to taste
- 1 cauliflower head, grated (or store-bought cauliflower rice)
- 1 red bell pepper, sliced
- 1 green bell pepper, sliced
- 1 onion, sliced
- 1 lime, juiced
- Fresh cilantro, for garnish

Instructions:

1. **Cook chicken** – Season chicken strips with cumin, chili powder, garlic powder, salt, and pepper. Sauté in olive oil over medium heat until fully cooked.
2. **Prepare cauliflower rice** – In a pan, sauté grated cauliflower with a little olive oil for 5–7 minutes, until tender.
3. **Sauté peppers and onions** – In the same pan, sauté bell peppers and onion until softened.
4. **Assemble bowls** – Layer cauliflower rice, chicken, sautéed veggies, and a squeeze of lime in bowls.
5. **Serve** – Garnish with fresh cilantro and serve warm.

Beef Stir-Fry with Veggies and Brown Rice

Ingredients:

- 1 lb flank steak, thinly sliced
- 2 tbsp soy sauce
- 1 tbsp hoisin sauce
- 1 tbsp sesame oil
- 2 garlic cloves, minced
- 1 cup broccoli florets
- 1 red bell pepper, sliced
- 1 carrot, sliced
- 1 cup cooked brown rice
- 1 tsp sesame seeds (optional)

Instructions:

1. **Marinate beef** – In a bowl, combine sliced beef with soy sauce, hoisin sauce, and sesame oil. Let marinate for 10–15 minutes.
2. **Cook veggies** – Stir-fry broccoli, bell pepper, and carrot in a hot pan for 3–5 minutes, until tender.
3. **Cook beef** – In the same pan, add marinated beef and garlic. Stir-fry for 3–4 minutes, until beef is cooked through.
4. **Serve** – Serve stir-fried beef and veggies over brown rice and sprinkle with sesame seeds if desired.

Veggie-Packed Lentil Soup

Ingredients:

- 1 cup dried lentils, rinsed
- 1 carrot, diced
- 1 celery stalk, diced
- 1 onion, chopped
- 2 garlic cloves, minced
- 1 can diced tomatoes
- 4 cups vegetable broth
- 1 tsp cumin
- Salt and pepper, to taste
- Fresh parsley, for garnish

Instructions:

1. **Sauté veggies** – In a large pot, sauté carrots, celery, onion, and garlic in olive oil until softened.
2. **Add broth and lentils** – Stir in lentils, diced tomatoes, vegetable broth, cumin, salt, and pepper. Bring to a boil.
3. **Simmer** – Reduce heat and simmer for 25–30 minutes, until lentils are tender.
4. **Serve** – Garnish with fresh parsley and serve warm.

Grilled Shrimp and Avocado Salad

Ingredients:

- 1 lb shrimp, peeled and deveined
- 1 tbsp olive oil
- 1 tsp chili powder
- 1 tsp garlic powder
- Salt and pepper, to taste
- 1 avocado, diced
- 1 cucumber, diced
- 2 cups mixed greens
- 1 lime, juiced
- Fresh cilantro, for garnish

Instructions:

1. **Grill shrimp** – Toss shrimp with olive oil, chili powder, garlic powder, salt, and pepper. Grill for 2–3 minutes per side, until pink and cooked through.
2. **Prepare salad** – In a bowl, combine mixed greens, avocado, cucumber, and grilled shrimp.
3. **Dress** – Drizzle with lime juice and garnish with fresh cilantro.
4. **Serve** – Serve immediately as a light and fresh salad.

Roasted Chicken with Sweet Potato and Broccoli

Ingredients:

- 2 chicken breasts
- 2 medium sweet potatoes, peeled and cubed
- 1 cup broccoli florets
- 2 tbsp olive oil
- 1 tsp paprika
- 1 tsp garlic powder
- Salt and pepper, to taste

Instructions:

1. **Preheat oven** – Set to 400°F (200°C).
2. **Prepare chicken** – Season chicken breasts with olive oil, paprika, garlic powder, salt, and pepper.
3. **Roast vegetables** – Toss sweet potato cubes and broccoli with olive oil, salt, and pepper. Spread on a baking sheet.
4. **Roast chicken and veggies** – Place chicken on the same sheet and roast for 25–30 minutes, until chicken is fully cooked and veggies are tender.
5. **Serve** – Serve warm with a side of roasted sweet potatoes and broccoli.

Chickpea and Quinoa Salad

Ingredients:

- 1 cup cooked quinoa
- 1 can chickpeas, drained and rinsed
- 1 cucumber, diced
- 1 bell pepper, diced
- ½ red onion, finely chopped
- 2 tbsp olive oil
- 1 tbsp lemon juice
- 1 tsp cumin
- Salt and pepper, to taste
- Fresh parsley, chopped

Instructions:

1. **Prepare quinoa** – Cook quinoa according to package instructions and let cool.
2. **Combine ingredients** – In a large bowl, combine quinoa, chickpeas, cucumber, bell pepper, and red onion.
3. **Make dressing** – Whisk together olive oil, lemon juice, cumin, salt, and pepper.
4. **Assemble salad** – Drizzle dressing over the salad, toss, and garnish with fresh parsley.
5. **Serve** – Serve chilled or at room temperature.

Tofu Stir-Fry with Veggies

Ingredients:

- 1 block firm tofu, pressed and cubed
- 1 tbsp sesame oil
- 1 cup broccoli florets
- 1 red bell pepper, sliced
- 1 carrot, sliced
- 2 garlic cloves, minced
- 2 tbsp soy sauce
- 1 tbsp rice vinegar
- 1 tsp honey
- 1 tsp sesame seeds (optional)

Instructions:

1. **Prepare tofu** – Sauté cubed tofu in sesame oil over medium heat for 5–7 minutes until crispy and golden. Remove and set aside.
2. **Cook veggies** – In the same pan, add more sesame oil and stir-fry broccoli, bell pepper, carrot, and garlic for 5–7 minutes.
3. **Make sauce** – In a bowl, whisk together soy sauce, rice vinegar, and honey.
4. **Combine** – Add tofu back to the pan and pour sauce over the vegetables and tofu, stirring to coat.
5. **Serve** – Garnish with sesame seeds and serve over rice or noodles.

Zucchini Noodles with Pesto and Chicken

Ingredients:

- 2 zucchinis, spiralized into noodles
- 2 chicken breasts, grilled and sliced
- 2 tbsp olive oil
- 1 cup basil pesto
- Salt and pepper, to taste
- Fresh Parmesan, for garnish

Instructions:

1. **Prepare zucchini noodles** – Heat olive oil in a pan and sauté zucchini noodles for 2–3 minutes until tender.
2. **Cook chicken** – Grill chicken breasts, season with salt and pepper, and slice into strips.
3. **Combine** – Toss zucchini noodles with pesto and top with grilled chicken.
4. **Serve** – Garnish with freshly grated Parmesan and serve immediately.

Grilled Turkey Burgers with Roasted Veggies

Ingredients:

- 1 lb ground turkey
- 1 tsp garlic powder
- 1 tsp onion powder
- Salt and pepper, to taste
- 1 tbsp olive oil
- 2 cups mixed veggies (zucchini, bell peppers, onions)

Instructions:

1. **Prepare turkey burgers** – Mix ground turkey with garlic powder, onion powder, salt, and pepper. Form into patties.
2. **Grill burgers** – Grill turkey burgers for 5–7 minutes per side, until fully cooked.
3. **Roast veggies** – Toss mixed veggies with olive oil, salt, and pepper. Roast in the oven at 400°F (200°C) for 20 minutes, stirring halfway through.
4. **Serve** – Serve turkey burgers with roasted veggies on the side.

Mediterranean Tuna Salad

Ingredients:

- 1 can tuna in olive oil, drained
- 1 cup cherry tomatoes, halved
- ½ cucumber, diced
- ¼ red onion, thinly sliced
- 2 tbsp Kalamata olives, chopped
- 1 tbsp olive oil
- 1 tbsp red wine vinegar
- Salt and pepper, to taste
- Fresh parsley, chopped

Instructions:

1. **Prepare salad** – In a bowl, combine tuna, cherry tomatoes, cucumber, red onion, and olives.
2. **Make dressing** – Whisk together olive oil, red wine vinegar, salt, and pepper.
3. **Toss** – Pour dressing over the salad and toss gently.
4. **Serve** – Garnish with fresh parsley and serve chilled or at room temperature.

Spaghetti Squash with Turkey Bolognese

Ingredients:

- 1 spaghetti squash, halved and seeds removed
- 1 lb ground turkey
- 1 onion, chopped
- 2 garlic cloves, minced
- 1 can diced tomatoes
- 1 tsp dried oregano
- 1 tsp dried basil
- Salt and pepper, to taste
- Fresh Parmesan, for garnish

Instructions:

1. **Cook spaghetti squash** – Place squash halves cut-side down on a baking sheet and bake at 375°F (190°C) for 35–40 minutes, until tender.
2. **Make turkey bolognese** – Sauté ground turkey with onion and garlic in a pan until browned. Add diced tomatoes, oregano, basil, salt, and pepper, and simmer for 10–15 minutes.
3. **Combine** – Use a fork to scrape spaghetti squash into noodles. Top with turkey bolognese sauce.
4. **Serve** – Garnish with freshly grated Parmesan and serve warm.

Eggplant and Chickpea Curry

Ingredients:

- 2 eggplants, cubed
- 1 can chickpeas, drained and rinsed
- 2 tbsp olive oil
- 1 onion, chopped
- 2 garlic cloves, minced
- 1 tbsp curry powder
- 1 can coconut milk
- 1 tsp cumin
- Salt and pepper, to taste

Instructions:

1. **Cook eggplant** – Sauté cubed eggplant in olive oil over medium heat until soft and golden.
2. **Make curry base** – In the same pan, sauté onion and garlic until softened. Add curry powder, cumin, salt, and pepper.
3. **Add chickpeas and coconut milk** – Stir in chickpeas and coconut milk, and simmer for 10–15 minutes.
4. **Serve** – Serve curry with rice or naan, garnished with fresh cilantro.

Asian Chicken Salad with Peanut Dressing

Ingredients:

- 2 chicken breasts, grilled and sliced
- 4 cups mixed greens
- 1 cucumber, julienned
- 1 red bell pepper, sliced
- ½ cup shredded carrots
- 2 tbsp peanut butter
- 1 tbsp soy sauce
- 1 tbsp rice vinegar
- 1 tsp honey
- 1 tsp sesame oil
- Salt and pepper, to taste

Instructions:

1. **Prepare salad** – In a large bowl, combine mixed greens, cucumber, bell pepper, carrots, and grilled chicken.
2. **Make dressing** – Whisk together peanut butter, soy sauce, rice vinegar, honey, sesame oil, salt, and pepper.
3. **Toss** – Drizzle dressing over the salad and toss to coat.
4. **Serve** – Serve immediately for a light and refreshing meal.

Beef and Broccoli Stir-Fry with Brown Rice

Ingredients:

- 1 lb flank steak, thinly sliced
- 2 tbsp soy sauce
- 1 tbsp sesame oil
- 1 garlic clove, minced
- 1 cup broccoli florets
- 1 cup cooked brown rice
- 1 tbsp oyster sauce (optional)
- Sesame seeds, for garnish

Instructions:

1. **Marinate beef** – In a bowl, combine sliced beef with soy sauce, sesame oil, and garlic. Let marinate for 10 minutes.
2. **Stir-fry beef** – In a hot pan, stir-fry beef until browned and cooked through. Remove and set aside.
3. **Cook broccoli** – In the same pan, stir-fry broccoli for 3–5 minutes until tender.
4. **Combine** – Add beef back to the pan with oyster sauce and toss to combine.
5. **Serve** – Serve beef and broccoli stir-fry over brown rice, garnished with sesame seeds.

Sweet Potato and Black Bean Tacos

Ingredients:

- 2 medium sweet potatoes, peeled and diced
- 1 can black beans, drained and rinsed
- 1 tbsp olive oil
- 1 tsp ground cumin
- 1 tsp chili powder
- Salt and pepper, to taste
- 8 small corn tortillas
- 1 avocado, sliced
- Fresh cilantro, for garnish
- Lime wedges, for serving

Instructions:

1. **Preheat oven** – Set to 400°F (200°C).
2. **Roast sweet potatoes** – Toss diced sweet potatoes with olive oil, cumin, chili powder, salt, and pepper. Roast for 25–30 minutes, until tender.
3. **Warm tortillas** – Heat tortillas in a pan or microwave.
4. **Assemble tacos** – Fill each tortilla with roasted sweet potatoes, black beans, avocado, and cilantro.
5. **Serve** – Serve with lime wedges for a refreshing touch.

Lemon Herb Grilled Chicken with Asparagus

Ingredients:

- 2 chicken breasts
- 2 tbsp olive oil
- Juice and zest of 1 lemon
- 1 tsp dried oregano
- 1 garlic clove, minced
- Salt and pepper, to taste
- 1 bunch asparagus, trimmed

Instructions:

1. **Marinate chicken** – In a bowl, combine olive oil, lemon juice, zest, oregano, garlic, salt, and pepper. Marinate chicken for 20–30 minutes.
2. **Grill chicken** – Preheat the grill to medium-high heat. Grill chicken for 6–8 minutes per side, until fully cooked.
3. **Grill asparagus** – Toss asparagus with olive oil, salt, and pepper, and grill for 5–7 minutes until tender.
4. **Serve** – Serve grilled chicken alongside asparagus for a healthy, flavorful meal.

Roasted Cauliflower and Lentil Bowls

Ingredients:

- 1 head of cauliflower, cut into florets
- 1 cup cooked lentils
- 2 tbsp olive oil
- 1 tsp turmeric
- 1 tsp ground cumin
- Salt and pepper, to taste
- 1 cup spinach, chopped
- 1 tbsp tahini (optional)

Instructions:

1. **Preheat oven** – Set to 400°F (200°C).
2. **Roast cauliflower** – Toss cauliflower florets with olive oil, turmeric, cumin, salt, and pepper. Roast for 25–30 minutes, until golden and tender.
3. **Assemble bowls** – In bowls, layer cooked lentils, roasted cauliflower, and fresh spinach.
4. **Serve** – Drizzle with tahini (if desired) and serve warm.

Chicken Caesar Salad with Greek Yogurt Dressing

Ingredients:

- 2 chicken breasts, grilled and sliced
- 4 cups Romaine lettuce, chopped
- ½ cup Parmesan cheese, grated
- 1 cup whole wheat croutons
- ½ cup Greek yogurt
- 2 tbsp lemon juice
- 1 tbsp Dijon mustard
- 1 tsp garlic powder
- Salt and pepper, to taste

Instructions:

1. **Grill chicken** – Season chicken breasts with salt, pepper, and olive oil. Grill for 6–8 minutes per side, then slice.
2. **Make dressing** – In a small bowl, combine Greek yogurt, lemon juice, Dijon mustard, garlic powder, salt, and pepper.
3. **Assemble salad** – In a large bowl, toss Romaine lettuce with sliced chicken, Parmesan cheese, and croutons.
4. **Serve** – Drizzle with Greek yogurt dressing and serve immediately.

Sweet Potato and Kale Breakfast Hash

Ingredients:

- 2 medium sweet potatoes, peeled and diced
- 2 tbsp olive oil
- 1 onion, diced
- 2 cups kale, chopped
- 2 eggs (optional)
- Salt and pepper, to taste

Instructions:

1. **Cook sweet potatoes** – Heat olive oil in a skillet over medium heat. Add sweet potato cubes and cook for 10–15 minutes until tender.
2. **Sauté onions and kale** – Add diced onion to the skillet and sauté for 2–3 minutes. Stir in chopped kale and cook until wilted.
3. **Cook eggs** – In a separate pan, fry or scramble eggs if using.
4. **Serve** – Top the hash with eggs and serve warm.

Grilled Steak and Veggie Skewers

Ingredients:

- 1 lb flank steak, cut into cubes
- 1 red bell pepper, chopped
- 1 zucchini, sliced
- 1 red onion, chopped
- 2 tbsp olive oil
- 1 tbsp soy sauce
- 1 tsp garlic powder
- Salt and pepper, to taste

Instructions:

1. **Marinate steak** – In a bowl, combine olive oil, soy sauce, garlic powder, salt, and pepper. Marinate steak cubes for 20–30 minutes.
2. **Prepare veggies** – Thread steak and vegetables onto skewers, alternating the ingredients.
3. **Grill skewers** – Preheat grill to medium-high heat. Grill skewers for 4–5 minutes per side, until steak is cooked to desired doneness.
4. **Serve** – Serve the skewers with a side of rice or quinoa.

Quinoa and Black Bean Burrito Bowls

Ingredients:

- 1 cup cooked quinoa
- 1 can black beans, drained and rinsed
- 1 cup corn kernels
- 1 avocado, sliced
- 1 lime, juiced
- 1 tbsp olive oil
- 1 tsp cumin
- Salt and pepper, to taste
- Fresh cilantro, for garnish

Instructions:

1. **Prepare quinoa** – Cook quinoa according to package instructions and let cool.
2. **Sauté vegetables** – In a pan, sauté corn with olive oil, cumin, salt, and pepper for 5–7 minutes.
3. **Assemble bowls** – In bowls, layer quinoa, black beans, sautéed corn, and avocado.
4. **Serve** – Squeeze lime juice over the bowls, garnish with fresh cilantro, and serve.

Spicy Chickpea and Sweet Potato Salad

Ingredients:

- 2 medium sweet potatoes, peeled and cubed
- 1 can chickpeas, drained and rinsed
- 1 tbsp olive oil
- 1 tsp smoked paprika
- ½ tsp cayenne pepper
- Salt and pepper, to taste
- 4 cups mixed greens
- 1 tbsp tahini (optional)

Instructions:

1. **Preheat oven** – Set to 400°F (200°C).
2. **Roast sweet potatoes and chickpeas** – Toss sweet potato cubes and chickpeas with olive oil, smoked paprika, cayenne, salt, and pepper. Roast for 25–30 minutes.
3. **Assemble salad** – In a large bowl, toss mixed greens with roasted sweet potatoes and chickpeas.
4. **Serve** – Drizzle with tahini (if desired) and serve warm.

Grilled Veggie and Tofu Wraps

Ingredients:

- 1 block firm tofu, pressed and sliced
- 1 red bell pepper, sliced
- 1 zucchini, sliced
- 1 tbsp olive oil
- 1 tsp garlic powder
- Salt and pepper, to taste
- 4 whole wheat wraps
- 2 tbsp hummus (optional)

Instructions:

1. **Grill tofu and veggies** – Toss tofu, bell pepper, and zucchini with olive oil, garlic powder, salt, and pepper. Grill for 5–7 minutes per side until charred.
2. **Assemble wraps** – Spread hummus (if using) on each wrap, then fill with grilled tofu and veggies.
3. **Serve** – Roll up the wraps and serve immediately.

Lemon Basil Chicken with Spinach and Rice

Ingredients:

- 2 chicken breasts
- 1 tbsp olive oil
- 1 tsp garlic powder
- 1 tbsp fresh basil, chopped
- 1 lemon, juiced and zested
- 2 cups fresh spinach
- 1 cup cooked rice
- Salt and pepper, to taste

Instructions:

1. **Season chicken** – Season chicken breasts with garlic powder, lemon juice, zest, basil, salt, and pepper.
2. **Cook chicken** – Heat olive oil in a pan over medium heat and cook chicken for 6–8 minutes per side until fully cooked.
3. **Sauté spinach** – In the same pan, add spinach and cook until wilted.
4. **Serve** – Serve chicken on a bed of rice, topped with sautéed spinach and a squeeze of fresh lemon.

Peanut Butter Banana Overnight Oats

Ingredients:

- 1/2 cup rolled oats
- 1/2 cup almond milk (or any milk of choice)
- 1/2 ripe banana, mashed
- 1 tbsp peanut butter
- 1 tsp chia seeds (optional)
- 1/4 tsp cinnamon
- Honey or maple syrup, to taste

Instructions:

1. **Combine ingredients** – In a jar or container, mix oats, almond milk, mashed banana, peanut butter, chia seeds, and cinnamon.
2. **Refrigerate** – Cover and refrigerate overnight or for at least 4 hours.
3. **Serve** – In the morning, top with additional banana slices, honey, or maple syrup if desired.

Spicy Turkey and Rice Bowls

Ingredients:

- 1 lb ground turkey
- 1 tbsp olive oil
- 1 tsp cumin
- 1 tsp chili powder
- ½ tsp cayenne pepper
- 1 cup cooked rice
- 1 cup black beans, drained and rinsed
- 1 avocado, sliced
- Fresh cilantro, for garnish

Instructions:

1. **Cook turkey** – Heat olive oil in a pan over medium heat. Cook ground turkey with cumin, chili powder, cayenne, salt, and pepper until browned.
2. **Assemble bowls** – In bowls, layer rice, black beans, cooked turkey, and sliced avocado.
3. **Serve** – Garnish with fresh cilantro and serve with a squeeze of lime.

Salmon with Roasted Brussels Sprouts

Ingredients:

- 2 salmon fillets
- 2 tbsp olive oil
- 1 tsp garlic powder
- 1 tbsp fresh lemon juice
- 1 lb Brussels sprouts, trimmed and halved
- Salt and pepper, to taste

Instructions:

1. **Preheat oven** – Set to 400°F (200°C).
2. **Prepare salmon** – Drizzle salmon fillets with olive oil, lemon juice, garlic powder, salt, and pepper.
3. **Roast Brussels sprouts** – Toss Brussels sprouts with olive oil, salt, and pepper. Spread on a baking sheet.
4. **Cook salmon and sprouts** – Roast salmon and Brussels sprouts for 20–25 minutes, until the salmon flakes easily and sprouts are tender.
5. **Serve** – Serve the salmon alongside roasted Brussels sprouts.

Baked Falafel with Tzatziki and Cucumber Salad

Ingredients:

- 1 can chickpeas, drained and rinsed
- 1/4 cup fresh parsley, chopped
- 2 garlic cloves, minced
- 1 tsp cumin
- 1 tsp coriander
- 1 tbsp olive oil
- 1/4 cup whole wheat flour
- 1/2 tsp salt
- 1/2 tsp pepper
- 1/2 cup tzatziki sauce
- 1 cucumber, diced
- 1 tbsp fresh dill, chopped

Instructions:

1. **Make falafel** – In a food processor, blend chickpeas, parsley, garlic, cumin, coriander, olive oil, flour, salt, and pepper. Form into small balls.
2. **Bake falafel** – Preheat oven to 375°F (190°C). Place falafel on a baking sheet and bake for 20 minutes, flipping halfway through.
3. **Prepare salad** – Toss cucumber and dill with a pinch of salt and pepper.
4. **Serve** – Serve falafel with tzatziki sauce and cucumber salad on the side.

Chicken Shawarma Bowls with Hummus

Ingredients:

- 2 chicken breasts, thinly sliced
- 2 tbsp olive oil
- 1 tsp ground cumin
- 1 tsp paprika
- 1/2 tsp turmeric
- 1/2 tsp cinnamon
- Salt and pepper, to taste
- 1 cup cooked rice
- 1/2 cup hummus
- Fresh parsley, for garnish

Instructions:

1. **Marinate chicken** – In a bowl, combine olive oil, cumin, paprika, turmeric, cinnamon, salt, and pepper. Marinate chicken for 15–20 minutes.
2. **Cook chicken** – In a pan, cook marinated chicken for 6–8 minutes, until fully cooked.
3. **Assemble bowls** – In bowls, layer rice, cooked chicken, and hummus.
4. **Serve** – Garnish with fresh parsley and serve immediately.

Zucchini and Turkey Meatloaf

Ingredients:

- 1 lb ground turkey
- 1 zucchini, grated
- 1/2 onion, chopped
- 1 egg
- 1 cup breadcrumbs
- 1/4 cup tomato sauce
- 1 tsp dried oregano
- Salt and pepper, to taste

Instructions:

1. **Preheat oven** – Set to 375°F (190°C).
2. **Prepare meatloaf** – In a bowl, combine turkey, zucchini, onion, egg, breadcrumbs, tomato sauce, oregano, salt, and pepper. Mix until well combined.
3. **Bake meatloaf** – Form the mixture into a loaf and place in a baking dish. Bake for 35–40 minutes.
4. **Serve** – Let cool for 10 minutes before slicing and serving.

Grilled Portobello Mushrooms with Quinoa

Ingredients:

- 4 large Portobello mushrooms, stems removed
- 2 tbsp olive oil
- 1 tbsp balsamic vinegar
- 1 cup cooked quinoa
- 1/4 cup feta cheese, crumbled
- Fresh basil, for garnish

Instructions:

1. **Preheat grill** – Set to medium-high heat.
2. **Prepare mushrooms** – Brush mushrooms with olive oil and balsamic vinegar, then season with salt and pepper.
3. **Grill mushrooms** – Grill mushrooms for 5–7 minutes per side.
4. **Assemble bowls** – In bowls, layer quinoa and grilled mushrooms. Top with crumbled feta and fresh basil.
5. **Serve** – Serve warm as a hearty and flavorful meal.

Roasted Shrimp and Veggie Buddha Bowls

Ingredients:

- 1 lb shrimp, peeled and deveined
- 1 tbsp olive oil
- 1 tsp smoked paprika
- 1 tsp garlic powder
- Salt and pepper, to taste
- 1 cup cooked quinoa
- 1 cup roasted veggies (carrots, broccoli, bell peppers, etc.)
- 1 avocado, sliced
- Fresh lemon, for garnish

Instructions:

1. **Preheat oven** – Set to 400°F (200°C).
2. **Roast shrimp** – Toss shrimp with olive oil, smoked paprika, garlic powder, salt, and pepper. Roast on a baking sheet for 6–8 minutes.
3. **Assemble bowls** – In bowls, layer quinoa, roasted veggies, and roasted shrimp.
4. **Serve** – Top with avocado slices and garnish with lemon wedges.

Turkey Chili with Quinoa

Ingredients:

- 1 lb ground turkey
- 1 onion, chopped
- 2 garlic cloves, minced
- 1 can diced tomatoes
- 1 can kidney beans, drained and rinsed
- 1 cup cooked quinoa
- 1 tbsp chili powder
- 1 tsp cumin
- Salt and pepper, to taste

Instructions:

1. **Cook turkey** – In a pot, cook ground turkey with onion and garlic until browned.
2. **Add ingredients** – Stir in diced tomatoes, kidney beans, quinoa, chili powder, cumin, salt, and pepper. Simmer for 20–25 minutes.
3. **Serve** – Serve warm, garnished with cilantro or a dollop of Greek yogurt.

Spinach and Ricotta Stuffed Chicken Breast

Ingredients:

- 4 chicken breasts
- 1 cup spinach, chopped
- ½ cup ricotta cheese
- 1 tbsp olive oil
- 1 tsp garlic powder
- 1 tsp dried oregano
- Salt and pepper, to taste

Instructions:

1. **Preheat oven** – Set to 375°F (190°C).
2. **Prepare filling** – In a bowl, mix spinach, ricotta cheese, garlic powder, oregano, salt, and pepper.
3. **Stuff chicken** – Cut a pocket into each chicken breast and stuff with the spinach and ricotta mixture.
4. **Cook chicken** – Heat olive oil in a pan over medium heat. Sear chicken on both sides for 2–3 minutes, then transfer to the oven and bake for 20–25 minutes.
5. **Serve** – Let chicken rest for a few minutes before serving.

Cauliflower Fried Rice with Tofu

Ingredients:

- 1 medium cauliflower, grated into rice-sized pieces
- 1 block firm tofu, pressed and cubed
- 1 tbsp sesame oil
- 1 onion, chopped
- 1 carrot, diced
- 2 garlic cloves, minced
- 2 tbsp soy sauce
- 1 tbsp rice vinegar
- 1/2 cup frozen peas
- 1 green onion, sliced (for garnish)

Instructions:

1. **Prepare cauliflower rice** – Grate cauliflower into rice-sized pieces using a box grater or food processor.
2. **Cook tofu** – In a pan, heat sesame oil and sauté tofu cubes until golden and crispy. Remove and set aside.
3. **Stir-fry vegetables** – In the same pan, sauté onion, carrot, and garlic for 5 minutes, then add peas and cauliflower rice. Cook for an additional 5–7 minutes.
4. **Add tofu and sauce** – Stir in tofu, soy sauce, and rice vinegar. Cook for 2–3 more minutes.
5. **Serve** – Garnish with green onions and serve warm.

Miso Soup with Tofu and Veggies

Ingredients:

- 4 cups vegetable broth
- 2 tbsp miso paste
- 1 block tofu, cubed
- 1 cup mushrooms, sliced
- 1 cup spinach, chopped
- 2 green onions, sliced
- 1 tbsp soy sauce
- 1 tsp sesame oil

Instructions:

1. **Prepare broth** – In a pot, bring vegetable broth to a simmer.
2. **Add miso paste** – Whisk in miso paste until dissolved.
3. **Add tofu and vegetables** – Add tofu, mushrooms, and spinach. Simmer for 5–7 minutes, until the vegetables are tender.
4. **Season** – Stir in soy sauce and sesame oil.
5. **Serve** – Ladle soup into bowls and garnish with green onions.

Thai Peanut Chicken with Veggie Noodles

Ingredients:

- 2 chicken breasts, grilled and sliced
- 2 zucchinis, spiralized into noodles
- 1 red bell pepper, sliced
- 1 carrot, julienned
- 2 tbsp peanut butter
- 2 tbsp soy sauce
- 1 tbsp lime juice
- 1 tsp honey
- 1 tsp ginger, minced
- Fresh cilantro, for garnish

Instructions:

1. **Prepare peanut sauce** – In a bowl, whisk together peanut butter, soy sauce, lime juice, honey, and ginger until smooth.
2. **Sauté veggies** – In a pan, sauté zucchini noodles, bell pepper, and carrot in a little oil for 2–3 minutes until tender.
3. **Add chicken** – Toss in grilled chicken slices and peanut sauce.
4. **Serve** – Garnish with fresh cilantro and serve immediately.

Roasted Beet Salad with Chickpeas

Ingredients:

- 2 medium beets, roasted and cubed
- 1 can chickpeas, drained and rinsed
- 4 cups mixed greens
- 1 tbsp olive oil
- 1 tbsp balsamic vinegar
- 1 tsp Dijon mustard
- Salt and pepper, to taste
- 1/4 cup feta cheese, crumbled

Instructions:

1. **Roast beets** – Preheat the oven to 400°F (200°C). Wrap beets in foil and roast for 40 minutes, until tender. Peel and cube.
2. **Make dressing** – Whisk together olive oil, balsamic vinegar, Dijon mustard, salt, and pepper.
3. **Assemble salad** – In a bowl, combine mixed greens, roasted beets, chickpeas, and feta.
4. **Serve** – Drizzle with dressing and serve chilled.

Grilled Chicken with Roasted Broccoli and Sweet Potatoes

Ingredients:

- 2 chicken breasts
- 2 tbsp olive oil
- 2 cups broccoli florets
- 2 medium sweet potatoes, peeled and cubed
- 1 tsp paprika
- 1 tsp garlic powder
- Salt and pepper, to taste

Instructions:

1. **Preheat oven** – Set to 400°F (200°C).
2. **Prepare vegetables** – Toss broccoli and sweet potatoes with olive oil, paprika, garlic powder, salt, and pepper. Roast for 20–25 minutes.
3. **Grill chicken** – Grill chicken breasts for 6–8 minutes per side, until fully cooked.
4. **Serve** – Serve grilled chicken with roasted broccoli and sweet potatoes.

Chia Pudding with Almond Butter and Berries

Ingredients:

- 2 tbsp chia seeds
- 1 cup almond milk (or any milk of choice)
- 1 tbsp almond butter
- 1 tsp vanilla extract
- 1 tbsp honey or maple syrup
- ½ cup mixed berries

Instructions:

1. **Prepare chia pudding** – In a jar, combine chia seeds, almond milk, almond butter, vanilla extract, and honey. Stir well and refrigerate overnight.
2. **Serve** – In the morning, top with fresh mixed berries.

Veggie and Quinoa Stuffed Peppers

Ingredients:

- 4 bell peppers, tops cut off and seeds removed
- 1 cup cooked quinoa
- 1 cup black beans, drained and rinsed
- 1 cup corn kernels (fresh or frozen)
- 1 tomato, diced
- 1 tsp ground cumin
- 1 tsp chili powder
- 1 tbsp olive oil
- Salt and pepper, to taste
- ½ cup shredded cheese (optional)

Instructions:

1. **Preheat oven** – Set to 375°F (190°C).
2. **Prepare filling** – In a bowl, combine cooked quinoa, black beans, corn, diced tomato, cumin, chili powder, salt, and pepper.
3. **Stuff peppers** – Stuff the peppers with the quinoa mixture and place them in a baking dish.
4. **Bake** – Drizzle with olive oil and bake for 25–30 minutes, until the peppers are tender. If using cheese, sprinkle it on top in the last 5 minutes of baking.
5. **Serve** – Serve warm, garnished with fresh herbs or a squeeze of lime.

Sweet Potato and Spinach Salad

Ingredients:

- 2 medium sweet potatoes, peeled and diced
- 4 cups fresh spinach
- 1 tbsp olive oil
- 1 tbsp balsamic vinegar
- 1 tbsp honey
- ¼ cup feta cheese, crumbled
- ¼ cup pumpkin seeds or walnuts (optional)
- Salt and pepper, to taste

Instructions:

1. **Preheat oven** – Set to 400°F (200°C).
2. **Roast sweet potatoes** – Toss sweet potato cubes with olive oil, salt, and pepper. Roast for 25–30 minutes until tender and caramelized.
3. **Assemble salad** – In a large bowl, combine roasted sweet potatoes, spinach, feta, and pumpkin seeds or walnuts.
4. **Make dressing** – Whisk together balsamic vinegar and honey. Drizzle over the salad and toss to combine.
5. **Serve** – Serve the salad warm or at room temperature.

Roasted Lemon Garlic Shrimp with Couscous

Ingredients:

- 1 lb shrimp, peeled and deveined
- 2 tbsp olive oil
- 2 garlic cloves, minced
- Zest and juice of 1 lemon
- 1 cup couscous
- 1 ¼ cups vegetable broth
- Salt and pepper, to taste
- Fresh parsley, chopped (for garnish)

Instructions:

1. **Preheat oven** – Set to 400°F (200°C).
2. **Prepare shrimp** – Toss shrimp with olive oil, garlic, lemon zest, lemon juice, salt, and pepper. Spread them out on a baking sheet.
3. **Roast shrimp** – Roast shrimp for 8–10 minutes, until pink and cooked through.
4. **Prepare couscous** – Bring vegetable broth to a boil in a small pot. Stir in couscous, cover, and remove from heat. Let it steam for 5 minutes, then fluff with a fork.
5. **Serve** – Serve shrimp over couscous and garnish with fresh parsley.

Baked Salmon with Roasted Brussels Sprouts

Ingredients:

- 2 salmon fillets
- 1 tbsp olive oil
- 1 tbsp lemon juice
- 1 tsp garlic powder
- Salt and pepper, to taste
- 1 lb Brussels sprouts, trimmed and halved
- 1 tbsp balsamic vinegar

Instructions:

1. **Preheat oven** – Set to 375°F (190°C).
2. **Prepare salmon** – Place salmon fillets on a baking sheet. Drizzle with olive oil, lemon juice, garlic powder, salt, and pepper.
3. **Roast Brussels sprouts** – Toss Brussels sprouts with olive oil, salt, and pepper. Spread on the same baking sheet.
4. **Bake** – Bake salmon and Brussels sprouts for 20–25 minutes, until the salmon is cooked through and Brussels sprouts are tender.
5. **Serve** – Drizzle Brussels sprouts with balsamic vinegar before serving.

Spaghetti Squash Primavera with Grilled Chicken

Ingredients:

- 1 medium spaghetti squash
- 2 chicken breasts, grilled and sliced
- 1 tbsp olive oil
- 1 zucchini, sliced
- 1 red bell pepper, sliced
- 1 cup cherry tomatoes, halved
- 1 tbsp fresh basil, chopped
- Salt and pepper, to taste
- Parmesan cheese, for garnish (optional)

Instructions:

1. **Preheat oven** – Set to 400°F (200°C).
2. **Cook spaghetti squash** – Cut squash in half, remove seeds, and drizzle with olive oil, salt, and pepper. Place cut-side down on a baking sheet and roast for 30–40 minutes.
3. **Grill chicken** – Season chicken breasts with salt and pepper. Grill for 6–8 minutes per side until cooked through.
4. **Sauté veggies** – In a pan, sauté zucchini, bell pepper, and cherry tomatoes in olive oil for 5–7 minutes.
5. **Assemble dish** – Use a fork to scrape the spaghetti squash into strands. Toss with sautéed veggies and top with grilled chicken. Garnish with fresh basil and Parmesan.

Grilled Chicken and Veggie Kabobs

Ingredients:

- 2 chicken breasts, cubed
- 1 red bell pepper, chopped
- 1 zucchini, sliced
- 1 red onion, chopped
- 1 tbsp olive oil
- 1 tsp smoked paprika
- 1 tsp garlic powder
- Salt and pepper, to taste
- Wooden skewers, soaked in water

Instructions:

1. **Preheat grill** – Set to medium-high heat.
2. **Prepare kabobs** – Thread chicken, bell pepper, zucchini, and onion onto skewers. Drizzle with olive oil and season with paprika, garlic powder, salt, and pepper.
3. **Grill kabobs** – Grill the kabobs for 5–7 minutes per side, until the chicken is fully cooked and the vegetables are tender.
4. **Serve** – Serve the kabobs warm with a side of rice or quinoa.